FULL
CIRCLE
New Delhi, India

OSHO
STRANGER TO THE EARTH
Coordination : Swami Amano Surdham

Photographs : Osho Photo Services

First Paperback Edition, 1997
ISBN 81-216-0685-3

FULL CIRCLE

Published by
FULL CIRCLE
18-19, Dilshad Garden
G.T. Road, Delhi-110 095
Tel: 229 7792, 93, 94 Fax: 228 2332

Designing, Typesetting
& Print Production : SCANSET
18-19 Dilshad Garden, G.T., Road, Delhi-110 095
Tel: 228 2467, 229 7792, 93, 94 Fax: 228 2332

Printed at Nu-Tech Photolithographers, Delhi-110 095

PRINTED IN INDIA

OSHO MEDITATION SERIES

MONTH FIVE

Stranger to the Earth

FULL
CIRCLE
New Delhi, India

OSHO MEDITATION SERIES

MONTH ONE	**SURRENDER TO EXISTENCE**
MONTH TWO	**SAY YES!**
MONTH THREE	**LOVE IS A FREE BIRD**
MONTH FOUR	**LIFE IS A GIFT**
MONTH FIVE	**STRANGER TO THE EARTH**
MONTH SIX	**BE A LAMP UNTO YOURSELF**
MONTH SEVEN	**ALONE WE FLY**
MONTH EIGHT	**LIVE DANGEROUSLY**
MONTH NINE	**I TEACH FEARLESSNESS**
MONTH TEN	**BECOME ONE WITH YOURSELF**
MONTH ELEVEN	**A DEWDROP IN THE OCEAN**
MONTH TWELVE	**MEDITATION — AN ECSTASY**

Time demolishes the steps
we climb to reach the present.
There is no going back —
only going forward is possible,
forward and forward —
and the journey is endless!
There is no goal, no destination,
only resting places,
where the tents are dismantled
as soon as they are pitched.

Osho

Bhagwan Shree Rajneesh
is now known simply
as Osho.

Osho has explained that
His name is derived
from William James' word
'oceanic' which means
dissolving into the ocean.
Oceanic describes the
experience, He says,
but what about
the experiencer? For that
we use the word 'Osho'.
Later He came to find out
that 'Osho' has also been used
historically in the Far East
meaning
"The Blessed One, on whom
the Sky Showers Flowers."

MONTH FIVE

Stranger to the Earth

OSHO

FULL CIRCLE
New Delhi, India

INTRODUCTION

The words on the following pages are extracted from talks the enlightened master, Osho, has given to His disciples and to other seekers visiting His commune in Pune, India. Most of the photographs were taken within the commune: Osho with His disciples and guests, seekers meditating, working, or simply being.

It was Osho's suggestion that the reader will find the book of most significance if it is used in the following way — that is, on first waking up, to read the passage designated for each morning before one's mind becomes engaged in the day's activities.

It is said that the last thought in one's mind as one falls asleep is also the first thought on waking. Perhaps the majority of us fall asleep with minds crammed with images from a television drama, with worries about the day that has passed and anxieties about the day that is to follow. A good many of us have trouble entering sleep at all. The pieces selected for the evening have been specially chosen for the night-time.

This series of twelve books is divided into twelve months, of thirty-one days each. "Month One" need not necessarily be the beginning of the calendar year but is the first month you begin reading. The passages have been designed to be read chronologically rather than randomly, as Osho's understanding of life is developed through each month.

The books have been planned in such a way that each day has a particular theme, and the subject of the morning and evening complement each other.

The quotations used for the morning contemplations are stimulating, sometimes pithy, sometimes exuberant — always endorsing a lively, total participation in the day to come. By contrast, Osho's words for the evening remind the reader of the significance of relaxation, expansion, melting, letting go.

Reading these passages is in itself a form of contemplation because, as Osho has said, the words of a mystic are not part of any kind of theory to be accepted or refuted; the reader is not asked to be a follower or a believer. In fact, it is not even the words themselves that are of significance, but rather what the words convey.

He explains: "(The mystic's) words carry a silence around them, his words are not noisy. His words have a melody, a rhythm, a music, and at the very core of his words is utter silence. If you can penetrate his words you will come across infinite silence.

"But to penetrate the words of a buddha, the way is not analysis, the way is not argument, the way is not discussing. The way is falling in rapport with him, becoming attuned with him, being in synchronicity with him. In that attunement, in that at-onement, one enters into the very core of the master's words. And there you will not find any sound, any noise; there you will find absolute silence. And to taste it is to understand the master.

The meaning of the word is not important, remember, but the silence of the word.

"If what I am saying to you is becoming a reality in your life, who cares whether you remember my words or not? It is perfectly right not to remember them; any remembrance of the words will be an obstruction. Let only pure meaning spread to the deepest core of your being where words have no access, where only wordless meaning is able to enter."

In fact, reading His words is more like listening to music than doing any mental exercise. Listening to music — or wine-tasting: take a sip, smell the bouquet and allow the flavor to tickle your spiritual palate.

Ma Prem Maneesha
Pune, India

OSHO MEDITATION SERIES

MONTH FIVE

OPEN
YOUR DOORS & WINDOWS

M O N T H 5

Morning Theme

PLAY
WITH
LIFE

MONTH 2

Evening Theme

DAY 1

Life is an opportunity, an opportunity to realize yourself. One can miss it, many miss it; only a few very rare people fulfill it. And those few people who fulfill it are the ones who enter into their inner world. To go on remaining concerned about money, power and prestige is a sheer wastage. One's primary concern should be to know, "Who am I?" Don't feel contented till you have known it. Make a great decision at the innermost core of your being: "I have to attain it," because that very decision becomes a seed.

DAY 1

Unless existence dances in you there is no possibility of any dance. Unless existence rejoices in you there is no possibility of rejoicing.

Remove yourself so that you don't come in between you and existence. Put the ego, the very idea of 'I' aside and be utterly empty, receptive. And the moment your emptiness is total, the whole starts showering millions of joys and millions of flowers upon you. The splendor is infinite.

DAY 2

Life is a journey, a pilgrimage. It is not static, it is dynamic. It is always moving towards the unknown. But because of our fear we cling to the known and do not allow life to move, do not give it enough freedom to go rushing towards the unknown, to go dancing towards the ocean. It is like a river, but we make it a pond. And to become a pond is a death. To remain a river is to remain alive. Ponds never reach anywhere. They only dry up; they become muddier and dirtier and they stink because they are stagnant. They can't remain fresh, they can't remain pure. The river remains pure, fresh, flowing. And there is joy because there is always a surprise awaiting you, there is wonder — what is going to happen next?

Every moment life is a surprise, a nonending surprise, a nonending suspense, a mystery which knows no beginning and no end. But one should remain a river; one should go on moving towards the ocean without any fear, without any clinging. Remain flowing, never allowing yourself to become stagnant —

DAY 2

remaining dynamic, young. The body is bound to become old one day but the spirit need not be old. It becomes old only if we allow it to become old. Death does not come as an end but only as a beginning; a new door opens up.

Consecrated to god is exactly the definition of sannyas. One starts living not for the ego but for the whole, one starts living as a vehicle of god, one becomes just like a hollow bamboo so that god can transform one into a flute. One empties oneself of oneself.

That's all that needs to be done: one has to empty oneself of oneself. And when one is empty something mysterious starts happening, unexplainable. Something of the beyond starts descending in you, some unknown force starts singing through you, dancing through you. That unknown force is god. God is not a person; it is only a name for all that is mysterious, for all that is beyond comprehension, for all that intellect is incapable of understanding. And to be consecrated to the miraculous, to the mysterious, is the only way to live a beautiful, graceful life. Otherwise people are only dragging themselves. Their life is not a dance, it cannot be.

DAY 3

Man only thinks that he dies; death is a fallacy. No one has ever died and no one has ever been born. Birth and death are both episodes in eternal life. Birth is not the beginning and death is not the end. You were before birth and you will be after death. To remember it, to realize it is the whole purpose of religion. To experience immortality is the only way to get rid of all fears and anxieties, because they are all rooted in the fear of death. Once you know there is no death and no birth you are free from fear, you are free from hell. You are free from all kinds of nightmares. A great peace settles in, and that peace is not the peace of a cemetery, it is a peace which sings and dances and celebrates. It is a peace full of life.

DAY 3

All that is great is always a gift of existence. It is never our achievement; in fact it happens only when we are utterly absent. Love happens when you are absent, truth happens when you are absent, bliss happens when you are absent. When you are too full of yourself nothing happens. Then gifts go on coming but you are not ready to receive them. The ego is very nonreceptive. We can receive existence's gifts only when we are utterly empty; the emptier you are the better. Existence is not miserly. It gives, and it gives much. It is willing to give everything, but we are not ready to receive. We don't have any space to receive its gifts. So start emptying yourself and you will be moving on the right way.

DAY 4

Meditation is only a way, a method, a technique to discover your way back home. It is inside you. It has always been there and it will always be there. You can go on wandering everywhere, you will remain in darkness unless you come back to your own being, unless you turn in and see your own self. The moment you see yourself all is light. And from that moment there is no darkness, no blindness. Everything is as clear as it can be. All problems disappear. Life becomes a sheer celebration.

Meditate more and more. Make it a point that whenever you have time, you give it to meditation. The first preference should be meditation.

DAY 4

The god of meditation is the only true god. All other gods are inventions — inventions of crafty priests, inventions of greedy minds, inventions out of fear. The only true god, which is not an invention, is experienced through meditation, because meditation requires you first to drop all thoughts, including thoughts about god.

When all thoughts and desires have been dropped, then whatsoever you have come to know is not part of your mind because we have put the mind aside from the very beginning. Now there is nobody to invent anything. Now you will know that which is.

DAY 5

Those who are knowledgeable will have to put their knowledge aside if they really want to become wise. It is not ignorance that hinders wisdom, it is knowledge that hinders wisdom; hence knowledge is real ignorance. All that you know is not real knowing; it is not your knowing, hence it is not real knowing. Put it aside — it is all garbage — so that you can know.

You are looking through others' eyes — how can you see? You cannot see through my eyes; that is impossible. You have your own eyes to see. And it is true not only for the outer eyes, it is also true for the inner eyes. You cannot live in a borrowed way — and that's what people are doing. That's why their life is just an imitation, a carbon copy. It has no beauty, no joy. You can't see any dance in it, any celebration in it. Only the original dances, sings, because only when you are original do you rejoice.

Man tries in every possible way to achieve bliss, by accumulating money, by becoming powerful, by becoming respectable, by becoming knowledgeable. But all these ways are doomed to fail. They cannot bring bliss to you. Bliss comes only in one way and that is by your becoming more conscious. The more you are conscious, the more you are blissful; the less conscious, the more miserable.

An consciousness becomes bigger and unconsciousness shrinks, you become blissful, more and more blissful. You start opening up like a flower. We are like buds, closed; as bliss comes you become a flower. In the East we say that one becomes a lotus, a one-thousand-petalled lotus. Everybody is carrying the seed, the bud, but great effort is needed to be conscious. Unconsciousness has been our habit for so many lives that it has almost become our nature. So from this moment try to be more and more conscious, in everything that you do, in everything that you think, in everything that you feel. These are the three dimensions. In all these three dimensions you have to become more watchful, more alert, more of a witness. Between these three arises

the fourth, the witness — and that is your true nature.

Once you have learned how to create the witness you know the secret art, you know the alchemy of transforming the dark continent in your being into light.

DAY 6

Every being is unique. God never creates carbon copies, he always creates originals. He believes only in the original. He is truly a creator, he never repeats. But man goes on living in imitation. We are trying to be somebody else — which is impossible. Whatsoever you do you are going to fail. You can only be yourself; there is no other possibility. But we are all trying to be somebody else. That is the whole story of our failure, the tragedy of life.

My work consists in helping you to respect yourself, to love yourself, to accept yourself and be yourself, because that's the only possibility; you cannot be otherwise. And there is no need to be otherwise — god has created you unique. I am not giving you a certain character or a certain style of life, but only an insight, an awareness, so that you can decide your lifestyle, so that you can live in your own light. And the moment you start living in your own light, bliss is yours.

When you do something creative a great contentment arises. When you finish a painting, a silence falls over you. You feel fulfilled, meaningful, significant, you have done something. You have participated in god's work. He is a creator and you have been a creator in your own way, a small way of course, but you have participated with god, you walked with god — maybe only a few steps, but you walked with god.

But the ultimate act of creativity is the flowering of your consciousness. After that you never leave god for a single moment. Then the whole pilgrimage is with him, within him. Naturally it is tremendously fulfilling. There can be no other fulfillment higher than that, greater than that. It is the very peak.

DAY 7

Prepare for the day; the sunrise has knocked on the door. Come out of your sleep. Don't go on hiding yourself under the blanket any more, howsoever cozy it feels and howsoever much your mind says, "Just turn over a little more, just a little more, a few minutes." Don't listen to the mind because those few minutes will never end, the mind always goes on postponing. It wants you to remain asleep because mind can exist only when you are asleep. When you are awake, mind disappears just like dreams disappear when you are awake. Mind is a dream phenomenon, made of the same stuff as dreams are made of. So no more postponement — wake up.

People go on doing a thousand other things rather than coming back home. If they are miserable they go on throwing responsibility on others. The wife is creating the trouble, the husband thinks that's why he is miserable... or the society or the state. There are a thousand and one excuses. One can always find them, they are always available. If you can't find them you can invent them. But no excuse is going to help, it simply prolongs your misery more. There is no excuse for your misery except the truth — and the truth is that you are very far away from your being.

So whenever you are miserable go into meditation: become silent, watch your misery; become a witness to it, don't become identified with it, and you will be surprised that the more you watch, the less it is. And when you are perfectly watchful it simply disappears, as if it has never been there. Not even a trace is left behind. And suddenly you will find that the same energy that was becoming your misery has become a showering of bliss. You have come home.

DAY 8

God is oceanic, infinite, unbounded. We have fallen apart because we have become identified with boundaries, with the boundaries of the body and the boundaries of the mind. These boundaries are keeping us away. Just get rid of these boundaries. I'm not saying to get rid of your body. The body is perfectly good, use it; it is your house, live in it. But don't think you are the body. You are in the body but you are not the body. You are in the mind but you are not the mind. And the moment you become disidentified with these boundaries, suddenly the gestalt changes, you start feeling unbounded. And that's what god is. You start becoming oceanic, vast.

Then there is no need to seek and search for god anywhere — you become it. And that is the only way to know god. The only way to know god is to become god. There is no other way. One cannot know god without becoming god.

Life is something tremendously beautiful but we are unaware of it, we are blind to it. It is glory, but we are not sensitive enough to receive it.

Life is perfect but our sensitivity is almost nil; hence the whole problem is how to create more sensitivity, how to become more alive, how to be more open, vulnerable, so that one can feel the life that surrounds us. The moment we are in step with life, life is god, and there is no other god.

And life knows no death, no birth. It is eternal, and we are part of that eternity. But we have gathered much rust around our mirrorlike being so that it reflects nothing. Our mind is like a layer of dust on our consciousness; hence nothing is reflected and we cannot see that which is. We only see the dust; we only see our thoughts, our desires, our memories, our dreams — and they are not the reality. Unless all this dust is cleaned away we will not be able to reflect that which is.

As one becomes more and more silent, peaceful, alert, sensitive, life becomes more glorious, more beautiful, more blissful. It is a great gift. But we are wasting time and opportunity, we are not appreciating that which has been given to us. We don't deserve it.

DAY 9

You are divine and you are formless. God is not something quantitative, god is only a quality. God is not something material. It is only a presence. It is not like a flower, it is more like a fragrance. One can feel it but one cannot catch hold of it. One can enjoy it, one can love it, one can dance with it, but one cannot possess it. One cannot put it in a bank, one cannot treasure it, because god is not one's property. That's the meaning of formlessness.

Never think of god as a person. Think of him only as a presence surrounding the whole existence. And then there is no need to go to any temple, to any statue. Wherever you are you can bow down in deep love and gratitude, you are connected with god. Whenever your heart is full of thankfulness and surrender, you are bridged with god.

We are all strangers on this earth. Our real home is on the other shore. We are here only to be ready to grow, to experience, to mature, so that we can be accepted on the other shore. We come into this life just as children are sent to school. It is a learning place, it is not our home. Learn as much as you can, experience as deeply as possible. Let your life be multi-dimensional, but remember one thing, that this is not our home. So don't get attached, don't become possessive, don't start clinging; otherwise who will go to the other shore? When the evening comes the child returns to his home. For the whole day he is in the school, in the evening he comes back. The school is a necessity; without it he cannot grow. With all its pleasures and pains, with all its foolishness and wisdoms, with all the joys and miseries we slowly slowly learn balancing, centering. Passing through many many agonies and ecstasies, something inside us matures, integrates. And when we are ready the boat arrives from the other shore to take us back home, but only when we are ready. Otherwise we are sent again and again, until we learn the lesson.

DAY 10

While you are reaching towards that inner flame, it is really an arduous path with many pitfalls. Moving in darkness one stumbles, moving in darkness one gets hit, moving in darkness one falls and has to rise again. One needs constant encouragement, one needs constant support, one needs somebody to prevent one from running away and escaping. That's the function of the master, to go on holding your hand, to go on telling you, "Don't be afraid — the goal is not far away — it is just around the corner." It is never around the corner, remember... but the master always says it is just around the corner. One day it is! But one has to wait for that day, one has to be patient.

I have heard a story of a great musician. He was singing a song, and the people who were listening to him were great lovers of music. He finished one song and the whole crowd said, "Again, once more." He sang it again, very happy that he had been received so well. When he finished it the whole crowd shouted even more loudly, "Again, once more!" He sang it again. When he finished for the third time the crowd shouted even louder. Then he said, "But I can sing other songs too." Then one person in the crowd said, "Until you sing it right, we are going to say, 'Again, again, again.'" That's what happens in life: we are sent again, again and again. You can die, but you will be sent back until you have learned the lesson. And the lesson can be learned.

DAY 11

The mediocre lives according to others; the intelligent person is one who lives according to his own light. Whatsoever the risk, he is capable of taking it because he relies on his own intelligence. He knows that the greater the challenge, the greater will be his intelligence; hence he accepts challenges. He lives in danger because intelligence grows only in danger, in insecurity. When there is no danger, no insecurity, intelligence dies. That's what I mean by a mediocre person: one who has allowed his intelligence to die, who has allowed his intelligence to gather rust. Meditation is the way to sharpen your intelligence more and more. And the more intelligence you have, the closer you are to god.

DAY 11

There are only two types of people in the world, those who complain and those who praise. The complainers remain miserable because their heart never opens up, never becomes a flower. Their very approach is negative. They only look at the darker side of things, they never look at the brighter side. They count thorns, they never praise the roses. When you start praising the beauty of the flowers and the silence of darkness and the joy of the river rushing towards the ocean, something starts opening up within you. You also start growing, you are no longer closed. The praise becomes a bridge between you and existence. You become more and more sensitive, more and more poetic, more and more aesthetic. Your sensibility makes you aware of the immense beauty that surrounds us, and of the great mystery which is unfathomable, which has no beginning and no end. The feeling that we are a part of this great mystery creates great rejoicing. Praise is prayer, and bliss is the fragrance of prayer.

DAY 12

Life is like a nightmare: if you are suffering in a nightmare all that you need is to put your total energy into waking up. Nothing else is needed. If you are being chased by a lion, you need not kill the lion because there is no lion at all. If you are being crushed under a rock, you need not remove the rock. It may be just your own pillow. All that you need is to wake up!

Without contributing to life nobody can ever feel blissful. So many people search for bliss but they fail for the simple reason that they are uncreative. They don't create anything. There is one joy and only one joy in the world, and that is of creating something, whatsoever that is: a poem, a song, a little music... whatsoever it is. But unless you create something you will not feel fulfilled. Only by creating something do you participate in god's being. God is the creator of the whole, and when you create a small thing, in a small way you become part of god. That's the only way to bridge the gap between you and god. No other prayer is going to help, no ritual is of any significance. They are just deceptive strategies invented by clever and cunning priests. The real prayer is to be creative. But how can you create it you don't know what your potential is, if you don't know in what direction you have to move so that you can become creative and can attain fulfillment? The work of meditation is simply to make you aware of your own potential. It simply throws light inside you, it focuses light on your inner being so that you can read the message.

DAY 13

Life is a gift, but very few people recognize it, because god goes on giving life without making any fuss about it. It is given so silently that we never become aware that something precious has been given to us. And god does not wait to be thanked. He does not make a show of it. He does not even whisper, "I am giving you the most precious thing in existence: life, consciousness, love." He really knows how to give. That is the art of giving: the person to whom the gift is given should not know about it; otherwise it will be a little humiliating, he may feel embarrassed.

Hence god gives anonymously, in such a way that the people who are receivers never become aware of the gift, unless they make a deliberate effort to be conscious of what has been given to them. And if you become conscious of it, you become capable of receiving more. If you become grateful for it, you become worthy of receiving more.

The person who thanks god for all that is happening to him goes on receiving more and more, because a thankful heart becomes more and more open, a thankful heart become more and more receptive. Remind

DAY 13

yourself that everything is a gift. Everything that has happened to you is a great gift — all the pains and all the pleasures, all the agonies and all the ecstasies, all the ups and all the downs. Everything is beautiful because everything is contributing towards your growth, towards your ultimate flowering.

Man is carrying within himself a tremendous capacity for music. When I say 'man' I mean every man. And when I say 'music' I don't mean ordinary music. Not everybody can be a musician in the ordinary sense. Only few have that talent. It is something inborn, innate.

My meaning of music is totally different. I mean the inner experience of harmony. It is far more musical than any music that can be created. It is uncreated music. No instruments are needed, no training of expertise is needed. All that is required of you to listen to it, is a deep silence. It is already there. It is your very life. The Zen people call it the sound of one hand clapping.

In ordinary music there are always two things needed, only then can sound be created. If you are playing a guitar then you have to use your hands on the strings. Only through the tension created by your fingers will the strings create music. But the inner music is something which is already there from the very beginning. It is just like your heartbeat; a little deeper than that, a little more mysterious than the heartbeat. It is the beat of your true heart.

DAY 14

God has no form, no name, no definition. God is indefinable, indescribable, inexpressible. Hence whatsoever has been said about god is all wrong. The moment it is said, it becomes wrong.

One can be right about god only if one remains silent. Utter a single word and you have missed the point. Nothing can be said about god, but god can be an experience. There is no proof, no logical certainty, but there is something existential.

Sannyas is a new way of looking at things. It is a way of looking at things in such a way that slowly slowly god starts emerging from everywhere. Although he has no form, he starts expressing himself in all forms possible; you start feeling him in all forms.

In one sense one wave is the ocean; in another sense every wave is the ocean. In one sense no form is god; in another sense every form is divine.

Mind cannot know because mind can only catch hold of forms. To know the formless you will have to go beyond the mind, you will have to drop the mind at least for a few moments every day, so that you can be

DAY 14

bathed with god. And those few moments are the real moments. These are the only moments that you have lived; all other moments will go down the drain, they will not be saved. Only those moments that you have lived with god, with the presence of god, are saved.

There have been two rivers of consciousness. One is of the philosophers — Aristotle in the West is the father of that, the originator. The other is of the mystics. That is a totally different kind of river. It has nothing to do with philosophizing, it is rooted in existential experience. And it has almost always happened that whenever there was a great mystic his followers always became divided between these currents.

The real ones, those who have understood the master, those who have really loved the master, became mystics. And those who have understood only the words of the master have become very knowledgeable; they became the philosophers.

Socrates was a mystic. Plato was his disciple but he lost track, he became a philosopher. Aristotle was Plato's disciple. So from this very moment remember: my way is the way of the mystic, not of a philosopher. I believe in bliss, not in theories about bliss. And I want you to taste it, not just to think about it. It is pointless to go on thinking about food — it won't nourish you. It is stupid to go on thinking about water. Why? — when

SAMADHI

the river is flowing, you can drink and quench your thirst. There are foolish people who are standing or sitting on the bank and thinking about water, theorizing about water, finding what water consists of and dying of thirst!

So don't be a thinker, don't be a philosopher, be a mystic. My sannyasins have to be mystics, existential experiencers. It is a part of realization.

DAY 15

The journey towards oneself needs great patience. But we have become so impatient. Particularly in this century man has lost the unhurried way of life. He is always in a hurry, he wants everything immediately. He thinks that everything is like instant coffee. But there are a few things which need great patience. Not that they cannot happen immediately; the paradox is that if you are patient enough they can happen immediately, instantly. But if you are in a hurry it will take infinite time for them to happen, or they may not happen at all. The impatient one may never get them and the patient one can get them immediately.

So this is to be understood from the very beginning of the journey, that it depends on you. If you are impatient the journey becomes very long; if you are patient the journey becomes very short. If you are absolutely patient, if you can say, "I am ready to wait forever," there may be no need to journey at all. Just sitting silently, doing nothing, spring comes and the grass grows by itself. It may happen like that!

Life should be looked at not as prose but poetry. That's the religious approach, the approach of the mystic. He looks, not with questions in his eyes, he looks with wonder, he looks with awe. He does not think about existence, he feels it. He opens his heart; rather than using his head he throws the doors and windows of his heart open, he allows the sun and the wind and the rain to come in. That's what I mean by poetry. The mystic is a poet in the ultimate sense. He may not write poetry — that is irrelevant — he lives poetry, he is poetry. Forget all about your head. Become headless and heartful. There are no problems in life; all problems are fabrications of the mind.

Life is a mystery to be lived, not a problem to be solved. Live it, enjoy it, sing with it, dance with it, play with it! Don't try to be philosophical, be poetic, and all joy will be yours. And you will be able to attain the ultimate treasure, the kingdom of god. It is available only to the poets.

DAY 16

Find time, space, and make it a point to meditate. In the beginning it is difficult, but remain patient; all that is needed is patience. And remain hopeful, optimistic, because it is only a question of time. It is as if you sow seeds; you can't expect the sprouts the next day. They will take their time, they will come only in their own time. They don't follow your expectations, they follow a certain law of their own. They have their intrinsic law, their own nature. They will wait for the right season, maybe for the clouds to come, for the rain, maybe for the spring....

So don't lose heart. That is one of the basic reasons why so many people start meditation and don't succeed. Many start but after just a few days they think, "I am not succeeding." It is not a question of succeeding or failing. Just go on doing it irrespective of what is happening — just as every day you take a bath, you go to sleep. You don't bother about whether you are succeeding or not, whether you are gaining something or not. A bath is good in itself, it has intrinsic value. Soon meditation becomes like an inner bath. You feel better, you feel more centered, more

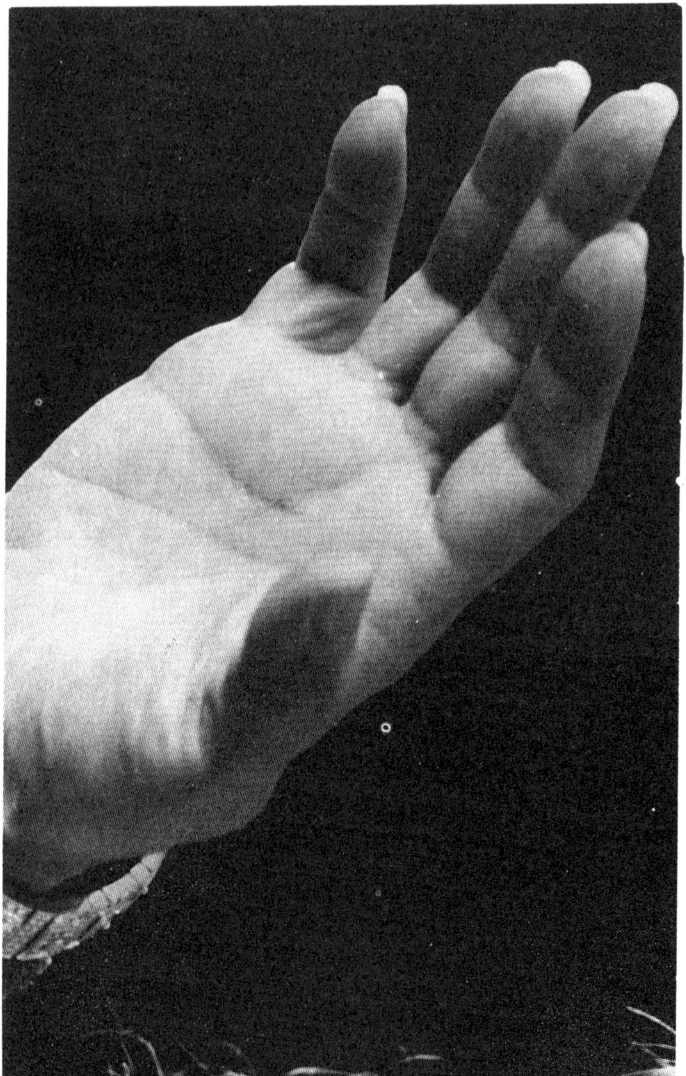

DAY 16

rooted, more grounded. And if one can keep waiting, one day suddenly it comes like an explosion, like lightning, and from that moment you are no more the same. From that moment you do not need to do meditation; then you are in meditation whatsoever you are doing. Then breathing is meditation, walking is meditation, eating is meditation. Then meditation simply becomes your very nature.

Everything that man has done to explain god has been destructive. Rather than making the world more religious, it has made the world less religious, because all these ideas are so inadequate that they can only satisfy fools. If you have a little intelligence then no religion can satisfy you. Just a little intelligence — not much! — then no religion can satisfy you. All religions have flaws, and such stupidities have been perpetuated. For example, the virgin birth of Jesus Christ.... That is a very essential thing, if you are to be a Christian. You have to believe in it. If you don't believe in it you are not a true Christian....

The real mystics have remained utterly silent about god, because the true god is known only in silence.

So drop all ideas of god and become more and more silent, and one day it is bound to happen: when the silence is total he comes so silently, so invisibly, that you are in for a great surprise. You don't hear his footsteps. One moment he was not there, the next moment he is there and you are overflowing with him. And you are no more the same person, and neither is the world the same.

DAY 17

Bliss is a sun that rises within you. Ordinarily man lives in a dark night, never knowing any dawn, never knowing any sunrise, just stumbling in the darkness, falling here, falling there, getting wounded. If you look at man's life, the whole life is simply a groping, and is of absolute futility because through this groping he never finds the door. The door can be found only if your inner being becomes full of light, if the sun rises. It happens through meditation. Meditation is the beginning of the sunrise. It is an invitation for the sun to rise within you. It is inviting light. It is inviting silence, peace. Ordinarily we never think of these things: peace, silence, stillness, light — and these are the real treasures. They constitute our real kingdom.

So from now onwards invite more and more peace, more and more silence, stillness. Don't miss a single opportunity to be silent, to be still. Don't miss a single opportunity to relax and look in. And one day it happens. It never happens gradually, it happens suddenly. You suddenly see the eastern hemisphere inside you becoming red; the sun is rising, the night is over. Then real life begins. Then each moment is so precious, so ecstatic, that each moment contains eternity. Then there is no past and no future, the present is all. Then one knows that one never dies, one is never born. One is always here and now.

Man is powerful when he is with existence. Whenever he is not with existence he is absolutely powerless. Plugged into existence you have infinite power; unplugged you are just empty. And unfortunately millions of people are living their lives unplugged; hence so much misery, so much feeling of impotence, so much feeling of emptiness, so much feeling of futility.

Everybody once in a while finds life utterly absurd. There seems to be no sense in it. One goes on living because one is afraid to commit suicide, one is afraid of death — at least one is acquainted with this empty life. One never knows what is going to happen in death and after death, so it is better to go on dragging yourself for the time being and hope for the best. But people are unplugged, that's the whole problem.

Religion simply means the art of getting plugged in to existence again. Then you are so full of power that it starts overflowing from you. You can share it and it is not exhausted. In fact the more you give it to others, the more you have it.

DAY 18

Go in, rest in your own being and slowly slowly as the rest becomes deeper, as your relaxation starts becoming a settled phenomenon, when nothing distracts you, when you become the center of a cyclone, then bliss arises. And of course, a blissful person is a blessing to the world, just as a miserable person is a curse to the world.

If one can remember only that one is divine it is enough of a meditation. If it becomes a constant remembrance just like an undercurrent in you, then nothing else is needed. And it is only a question of remembering that you are divine. When you remember that you are divine you naturally remember that everybody is divine. You can be divine only if everybody else is divine. You can be divine only in a divine existence. We are part of one organic unity.

So remember it as often as possible. Let it become like breathing and it will reveal many mysteries to you. When you are looking at people remind yourself they are all divine, and the trees and the rocks and the stars. And when you start feeling surrounded by thousands of divine forms, naturally it becomes impossible to be miserable. One simply feels as if one is flying. One becomes weightless, one starts growing wings. That is your meditation, that is your prayer.

We live in desire. Desire means discontentment. Desire means that whatsoever is, is not right, not enough: more is needed. And desire is never fulfilled. It is unfillable by its very nature.

You can have as much as you desire, but the moment you have it desire goes on jumping ahead of you, it starts asking for more. Its greed knows no limits, it is unlimited greed. It is like the horizon: it looks so close — you can reach it within an hour if you run. But you can never reach it. The distance between you and the horizon will remain the same, constantly the same, because there is no horizon; it is an illusion. The earth is not meeting with the sky anywhere, it only appears to be.

Such is the case with desire. It only appears that if I could reach to that point, if I could attain to this or that, there would be contentment. I would be happy, I would be fulfilled. But it never happens.

One has to understand desiring and its futility. In that very understanding desire disappears and one is left at home in deep peace. When there is no desire, there is no disturbance. Desire is the only disturbance.

DAY 19

Prayer is not scientific. But meditation is utterly scientific. Just as the scientist watches, observes the objective phenomenon, the meditator watches the psychological phenomenon. It is the same process: a detached watching, unprejudiced observation, with no conclusions — because if you have a conclusion already then there is no point in watching. Then you will manage to prove your conclusion, then the whole process is unscientific.

The same process of observation has to be turned towards your own mind. One becomes a lab, a great experiment of observation: one watches one's thoughts, desires, memories, anger, greed, lust, with no prior conclusion, with no judgment: this is good, this is bad... nonjudgmental.

When you are absolutely nonjudgmental, with no prejudice, no conclusion, when your observation is pure, simple, innocent, that which you observe starts disappearing. That's where science and religion start differing: the more you observe in science, the more real the fact becomes. It was not so real before observation. You may have missed it, but now

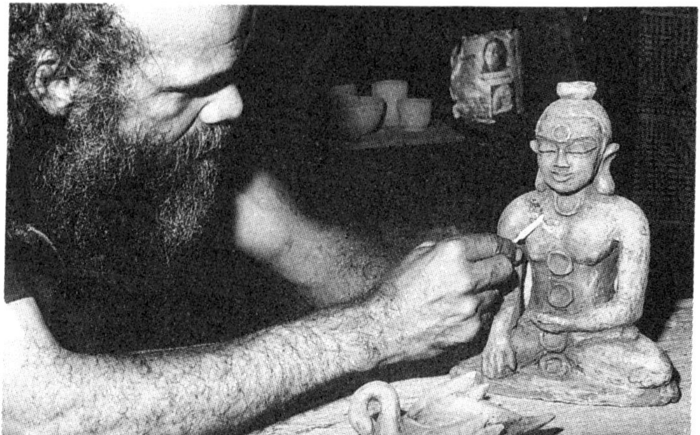

DAY 19

you cannot miss it; it is there, it becomes more solid. When you watch your mind this is the difference: if you watch your anger it starts evaporating, it cannot exist. Slowly slowly, the whole mind ceases to be. When there is no mind left to watch, the watcher turns upon himself.

That is the moment of realization, self-realization, samadhi. That is the ultimate goal of all mystical approaches.

DAY 19

Our desires are dreams, all our thoughts are dreams. And we go on continuously living in dreams because we are asleep. Dreams can exist only if we are asleep, and dreams disappear the moment we awake. Going beyond dreams means awaking.

It is time. You have slept enough, for many many lives. Don't miss this opportunity to wake up because rare is the opportunity, and to miss it is very easy. So put your whole energy into waking up. In the beginning it seems almost impossible — how to do it? But if one goes on trying... in sleep one tosses and turns, but if one goes on tossing and turning, It is bound to disrupt the sleep. And just a moment's glimpse of being awake is enough to trigger a new process in your being. Then more and more moments of awakening happen. And the day that one becomes fully awakened, twenty-four hours a day, even while one is asleep one remains alert, aware — when the body sleeps the soul never sleeps — when one is capable of being awake twenty-four hours a day even when the body is resting, then one should feel contented. One has arrived. Before that, make every possible effort that you can. Don't leave any stone unturned.

DAY 20

There is a feeling that existence is totally indifferent to us. It is not so. This is a stupid idea that has come into the mind of man because of scientific progress.

Science has given many blessings to man, but certain curses have also come in the wake of it. It has made man's body more healthy, more nourished, but it has made man's soul very undernourished, almost starving. It has given much, but it has also taken much; and what it has given is superficial, nonessential, and what it has taken away is the essential. So science goes on giving us a more comfortable life but at the same time a tremendous feeling of meaninglessness. Any intelligent person starts feeling that to exist is pointless. And the reason is not that it is pointless, the reason is that we have completely forgotten the language with which to relate to existence.

We are asleep not in the ordinary sense but in a metaphysical sense. We don't know who we are, how can we be called awake? We don't know anything that is essential. We know much that is rubbish — we know everything about the moon and the sun and the earth and we know history and geography — but we know nothing about ourselves. We know nothing about the knower — and that should be the primary concern of any real education....

Fundamentally you have to become aware of yourself, of who you are. And only you can do that.

I can call you forth but you will have to come out, you will have to gather enough courage to come out of the darkness, out of the centuries- old habits, out of a long long sleep.

And when you are awake, life is a dance, a song, a bliss, a benediction.

DAY 21

Remember it again and again: seeing the sky know that you are also the sky; seeing the stars know that the stars are within you. As such you are within the sky, the sky is within you. Slowly slowly, your whole gestalt will change and in that new gestalt small problems can't arise, they become ridiculous. That's how the real man of religion passes through life: unaffected, calm, cool and tranquil, centered and rooted in his being — nothing can make him waver, not even death, because even death cannot take anything away from him. He has dropped all that can be taken away and he has become one with that which is eternally abiding.

To be a man is a great gift, but very few people realize it. You could have been anything in this vast universe — a rock, a cabbage, a potato... anything! And there is no court of appeal! Whatsoever one is, one is; nothing can be done about it. What can the poor potato do about it? But very few people realize that they are human beings and that they have tremendous potential to grow. The beauty and the grandeur of being human is that it is only through being human that one can reach god. It is a first basic requirement. No other animal has any approach towards god, only man — and not even all men. Only people who are really alert and aware — those very few people create a bridge between themselves and god. Without that bridge life is meaningless and a great opportunity can be lost very easily.

DAY 22

Man is born only as an opportunity. He has great potential, but remember a potential is only a potential. It has to be transformed into a reality, it has to be actualized. And great effort is needed. It is an uphill task. One has to be industrious, one cannot attain to bliss by just hoping for it. Just desiring it is not enough. You have to put all your energies to the task. And it is the greatest achievement of life. Hence it needs your total commitment, less than that won't do.

DAY 22

There are many wrong ways towards god but only one right way. The wrong ways are: one can move towards god through fear. One will only think that one is moving, one will never move. That's why it is wrong. How can you go towards god if you are moving out of fear? The natural tendency when you are afraid is to escape. You can go away farther away from god, but not closer to him. And all the religions have been teaching people to be afraid of god. Religious people are defined as god-fearing. Now, that is ridiculous — a religious person never fears god, he loves him. Man can also move towards god through greed. That is the wrong way again, because greed means you want to exploit. Greed means you have certain desires to be fulfilled through god, god is not your goal. You want money, you want power, you want paradise, you want all the pleasures of paradise. And because that can be got only through god, out of compulsion you surrender to god. But god is the means, not the end, and to reduce god to a means is ugly, it is disgusting. God is

the ultimate end, there is nothing beyond it. And so on and so forth... these are the wrong ways. They appear to be ways but they are not ways they are walls. The only right way is love.

Love more, love deeply, love for love's sake, and you will be surprised that slowly slowly something new starts happening around you: the presence of god is felt.

DAY 23

Man can function in two ways. Either he can function as a thinking machine, just like a computer. That's what our schools, colleges and universities are preparing people for; to function as skillful, efficient computers. But then they destroy your soul. The computer can do anything that Albert Einstein can do, but the computer cannot become enlightened. It cannot do that which only a buddha can do. Humanity is dying, and dying so slowly that we are not even becoming aware of it. The death is happening through a very slow poisoning. Man is transformed more and more into a biocomputer.

The heart is your real center. Don't neglect it, don't be indifferent to it. Use the mind but don't be used by the mind. Use the mind as a beautiful machine — as a car, as a computer, as an airconditioner... but not more than that. Remain rooted in the heart, function from the heart. Let feeling be decisive. Howsoever illogical they appear, let them be decisive and your life will have a dance of its own, a beauty of its own, a bliss of its own, a benediction of its own.

DAY 23

Whenever you are in a loving space god fills it. And once you have tasted the joy of being filled with god you would like to remain in love twenty-four hours a day. Then love becomes your natural state and god becomes your inner experience. It is only through love that people have reached god. Others have been wandering astray. Love is my message, but don't cling to the word 'love', don't make a gospel out of it. It is to be experienced.

DAY 24

A divine voice is always there in the heart, always calling you. But you are not available, you are engaged in some mundane affairs, in some ordinary things. Your mind is full of unnecessary rubbish, busy without business. So you go on missing the still small voice within. Once the mind is silent, once thoughts disappear, once you are left without any thoughts, suddenly the voice is heard. And to hear god directly from your own heart is the beginning of transformation, it is a revelation. God always comes as a revelation, never as knowledge but always as revelation. Remember it.

And it is not far away. He is always there twenty-four hours a day, waiting for you. But people go on running hither and thither. They waste their whole life in such stupid nonsense that it seems unimaginable that man can be so unintelligent. But he is.

DAY 24

A heart full of love, loyalty, trust is exactly the definition of a religious consciousness. These qualities are needed. Without these qualities one can never become aware of god, of love, of beauty, of the tremendous splendor of existence.

Existence is known through the heart, not through the head, and the heart approaches existence in deep love, trust. There is no other way to commune with the whole.

These qualities slowly slowly transform you. They transform you from doubting confusion into an absolute certainty of knowing. They take you out of the chaos of the head into the harmony of the heart. Remember them.

DAY 25

The heart is always true. The heart is never untrue and the head is never true. The head lives in lies, it lives on lies, it exists in all kinds of falsehoods. The heart is authentic, it is sincere, it is simple, it is not cunning. It is tremendously intelligent but not cunning. It simply reflects that which is. That's its beauty and its truth. God is never known through the head. Anything that has any value is never known through the head. Love, beauty, god, they are all known through the heart. The heart is the gateless gate to reality. Move from the head to the heart.

Prayer does not mean saying something to god, asking for something, prayer means listening to god. If you have to say something it can only be a thank you. A simple yes is enough.

But organized religions all over the world have been teaching people unnecessary prayers. And people are repeating those prayers, parrotlike. They have lost all meaning, they have become pure ritual, they are only formal.

You have to learn the true prayer. It consists of silence, it consists of deep listening. God wants to convey something to you. He is searching for you, but he never finds you because you are always so busy.

Be silent, more and more unoccupied, more and more available, and you will soon start hearing the still, small voice within. God does not speak from the outside, he speaks from your innermost core, he is already there. And to be connected with your innermost core is true prayer. The moment you are connected... it is so blissful, so ecstatic that you can only bow down in deep gratitude.

DAY 26

It is tenderness that makes you vulnerable, that makes you open, that makes you sensitive to the mysterious that surrounds us. People who are not tender, who are hard like rock, go on missing life. Life passes by; it cannot penetrate them, they are impenetrable. Life is such a joy for those who are tender, soft, loving, compassionate, sensitive. Then life itself is proof; in thousands of ways it proves that god is. But to the hard, to the rocklike person, there is no proof for god. God cannot be proved for him because he has no sensitivity to feel. He has lost all feeling, he lives only in thinking. He has lost his heart, he is just a head. And the head is just rubbish. Be a heart! Even if you have to lose the head, lose the head — it is worth it. It is beautiful to be headless, but it is ugly to be heartless.

DAY 26

Worshippers are many, the world is full of them. Churches, mosques, temples, synagogues are all full of worshippers, but I don't call them worshippers. Their worship is only ritual. They are simply following a tradition. They are worshipping symbols. Their heart is not full of love, they don't really have a thirst for god; they are simply performing a social duty. Maybe they have become addicted to it, if they don't do it they feel something is missing....

I am not interested in rituals. I don't teach that you should say a particular prayer, that parrotlike you should repeat certain formulas in Arabic, in Hebrew, in Sanskrit — in some dead language, long-forgotten. I don't teach any gibberish. I simply teach you to love the beauty of existence that surrounds you. This is true worship because god is manifest; in thousands of ways he is available — in the trees, in the flowers, in the birds, in the mountains, in the sun, in the moon, in people, in animals. Feel him. Rather than believing, feel the beauty of existence, feel the splendor of the universe, the splendor of a night full of stars.

DAY 26

If a beautiful sunset cannot help you to bow your knees, then no temple, no church, is going to help you. If a distant call of a cuckoo has no magic for you then you are dead, then worship cannot happen to you. Worship can happen only when the heart is throbbing with life.

DAY 27

I don't divide ordinary life from spiritual life. They are one, they are inseparably one. To separate them is to create a split humanity, a schizophrenic humanity. Life is a unity, an organic unity, indivisible. Nothing is higher and nothing is lower. There is no hierarchy, everything exists simultaneously, on the same plane. So nothing has to be renounced, nothing has to be rejected. Of course everything has to be transformed and transformed through love, transformed through bliss, transformed through joy. If you can bring dance to your life, if each moment of your life can become a melody, if it can become a rhythmic experience, then god is bound to come to you.

Never be worried about what other people say about you, never take any note of it. Always think of only one thing: "God is my judge. Am I able to face god?" Let that be the criterion of your whole life and you will not go amiss.... One has to stand on one's own feet and the only consideration should be: Whatsoever I am doing should be according to my light. My consciousness should be the deciding factor. Then god is your judge.

DAY 28

Once you start trusting, you start opening up. In distrust one closes — naturally, in defense one closes, one is afraid to be vulnerable. In trust one opens up; there is nothing to fear, this is our home. The trees and the stars and the sun and the moon are all part of our family, our brothers and sisters. The universe is a family.

This experience is possible only when you trust — and after that, bliss is inevitable. Without it misery is our fate, it cannot be avoided. With it bliss is natural, it comes of its own accord.

DAY 28

Everyone is favored by god equally. There is no partiality in existence. Existence is absolutely impartial. But that does not mean that it is cold. It is very warm, loving, protecting, caring. But we are not open to its warmth, we are closed.

The problem is with us, not with existence. Hence the whole effort down the ages has been a single one: to help people to open up so that they can commune with the stars and the clouds and the sun and the moon — because this totality is what god is. There is no god other than this existence. And unless you are open, fearlessly open, you will never become aware of what you are missing. You are missing life, you are missing love, you are missing truth.

Gather courage and open yourself to all the beauty and the blessing and the benediction. It is all yours. Just for the asking it is yours.

DAY 29

Life can either be lived as a downhill phenomenon or as an uphill task. If you are moving downhill, it is convenient, comfortable. No effort is needed on your part, no risk, no challenge — but no gain either. You simply drift from birth to death. Life remains a vast emptiness. One needs to be industrious, one needs to accept challenges which provoke one for the upward journey. It is hard, it is dangerous, but it brings out the best in you. It creates integrity, ultimately it creates a soul in you. One has to put one's total energies to the task, only then... one has to risk all, only then... but then life blooms, flowers. It becomes a joy, a fulfillment, a contentment, a blessing.

Priests down the ages have condemned man so much that everybody feels rejected, everybody feels, "I am just junk." Slowly slowly the priests have destroyed all self-respect. They have created a division in every person: the condemned part and the condemner.

The condemner they call your conscience and the condemned part they call your instincts. This division keeps you in a constant quarrel with yourself, in disharmony. You are at daggers with yourself, and that is no way to know existence.

The first lesson is to love yourself as you are, because existence loves you as you are. That does not mean that you have to remain the same forever.

In fact this is the first step of transformation: if you love yourself you will be able to grow quicker, faster.

DAY 30

We are born with a great treasure, so vast, so great that it is inexhaustible. But we live in utter poverty because we never dig within our own being. We go on looking everywhere else. This is the most strange thing about man, that he searches and seeks everywhere — he is ready to go to Everest, he is ready to go to the moon — but he is not ready to go within.

The moment you say, "Go within," it falls on deaf ears. And it is there the treasure is. So we go on carrying the treasure with us and still remain beggars. Your reality is within and you go on searching and seeking without. The first inquiry should be made within. If you don't find it there, then of course you can go exploring the whole world. But that has never happened. Those who have gone within have always found it.

DAY 30

God is always with us; the problem is from our side, we are not with him. If god were not with us we could not exist even for a single moment. He is our life, he breathes in us, he beats in our hearts, he is our consciousness. He is always with us, but we are not always with him.

The moment we are also with him a radical change happens. Then you become aware of the meaning, of the significance of the song of life. Then you become aware of how much has been bestowed upon you, how much has been given to you. Then great gratefulness is felt, and that gratefulness is the essential core of religion, the very soul of religion. Everything else is ritual. To feel gratitude is to be religious.

DAY 31

The moment one starts seeking and searching for oneself one becomes the blessed one. The inquiry itself is the beginning of the transformation. The more passionate the inquiry is, the sooner the transformation will come. Make it intense, make it total.

This is one of the fundamental secrets of life and existence: you live only when you have something for which you are ready to sacrifice even your life. Life begins only when you have something more — higher, bigger, holier than life, in your life. When life itself becomes just a means to higher end, then your life starts having a context. And in that context only is there meaning, significance, joy.

DAY 31

This is the law of existence: truth cannot be conquered but can be invited. One has to be just a host for the ultimate quest. And that's what I call meditation: it simply makes you empty of all rubbish, it empties you completely so you become spacious, receptive, sensitive, vulnerable, available. And all those qualities make you passionately inviting — an invitation for the unknown, an invitation for the unnameable, an invitation for that which will make your life a fulfillment, without which life is just an exercise in utter futility. But one cannot do anything more than that: just an invitation and waiting.

This is what I call prayer: invitation and waiting in deep trust that it is going to happen. And it happens, it has always happened! This is the ultimate law of existence.

About Osho

Most of us live out our lives in the world of time, in memories of the past and anticipation of the future. Only rarely do we touch the timeless dimension of the present — in moments of sudden beauty, or sudden danger, in meeting with a lover or with the surprise of the unexpected. Very few people step out of the world of time and mind, its ambitions and competitiveness, and begin to live in the world of the timeless. And of those who do, only a few have attempted to share their experience. Lao Tzu, Gautama Buddha, Bodhidharma... or more recently, George Gurdjieff, Ramana Maharshi, J. Krishnamurti — they are thought by their contemporaries to be eccentrics or madmen; after their death they are called "philosophers." And in time they become legends — not flesh-and-blood human beings, but perhaps mythological representations of our collective wish to grow beyond the smallness and trivia, the meaninglessness of our everyday lives.

Osho is one who has discovered the door to living His life in the timeless dimension of the present — He has called Himself a "true existentialist" — and he has devoted His life to provoking others to seek this same door, to step out of the world of past and future and discover for themselves the world of eternity.

Osho was born in Kuchwada, Madhya Pradesh, India, on December 11, 1931. From His earliest childhood, His was a rebellious and independent spirit, insisting on experiencing the truth for Himself rather than acquiring knowledge and beliefs given by others.

After His enlightenment at the age of twenty-one, Osho completed His academic studies and spent several years teaching philosophy at the University of Jabalpur. Meanwhile, He traveled throughout India giving talks, challenging orthodox religious leaders in public debate, questioning traditional beliefs, and meeting people from all walks of life. He read extensively, everything He could find to broaden His understanding of the belief systems and psychology of contemporary man. By the late 1960s Osho had begun to develop His unique dynamic meditation techniques. Modern man, He said, is so burdened with the outmoded traditions of the past and the anxieties of modern-day living that he must go through a deep cleansing process before he can hope to discover the thought-less, relaxed state of meditation.

In the early 1970's, the first Westerners began to hear of Osho. By 1974 a commune had been established around Him in Poona, India, and the trickle of visitors from the West was soon to become a flood. In the course of His work, Osho has spoken on virtually every aspect of the development of human consciousness. He has distilled the essence of what is significant to the spiritual quest of contemporary man, based not on intellectual understanding but tested against His own existential experience.

He belongs to no tradition — "I am the beginning of a totally new religious consciousness," He says. "Please don't connect me with the past — it is not even worth remembering."

His talks to disciples and seekers from all over the world have been published in more than six hundred volumes, and translated into over thirty languages.

Osho left His body on January 19, 1990, as a result of poisoning by US government agents while held incognito in custody on technical immigration violations in 1985. His huge commune in India continues to be the largest spiritual growth center in the world attracting thousands of international visitors who come to participate in its meditation, therapy, bodywork and creative programs, or just to experience being in a buddhafield.

Books by Osho

ENGLISH LANGUAGE EDITIONS

EARLY DISCOURSES AND WRITINGS
A Cup of Tea
Dimensions Beyond The Known
From Sex to Superconsciousness
The Great Challenge
Hidden Mysteries
I Am The Gate
Psychology of the Esoteric
Seeds of Wisdom

MEDITATION
And Now and Here (Vol 1 & 2)
In Search of the Miraculous (Vol 1 & 2)
Meditation: The Art of Ecstasy
Meditation: The First and Last Freedom
Vigyan Bhairav Tantra *(boxed 2-volume set with 112 meditation cards)*
Yaa-Hoo! The Mystic Rose

BUDDHA AND BUDDHIST MASTERS
The Dhammapada (Vol 1-12) *The Way of the Buddha*
The Diamond Sutra
The Discipline of Transcendence (Vol 1-4)
The Heart Sutra: The Book of Wisdom *(combined edition of Vol 1 & 2)*

BAUL MYSTICS
The Beloved (Vol. 1 & 2)

KABIR
The Divine Melody
Ecstasy: The Forgotten Language
The Fish in the Sea is Not Thirsty
The Great Secret
The Guest
The Path of Love
The Revolution

JESUS AND CHRISTIAN MYSTICS
Come Follow to You (Vol 1-4)
I Say Unto You (Vol 1 & 2)
The Mustard Seed
Theologia Mystica

JEWISH MYSTICS
The Art of Dying
The True Sage

SUFISM
Just Like That
Journey to the Heart (same as Until You Die)
The Perfect Master (Vol 1 & 2)
The Secret
Sufis: The People of the Path (Vol 1 & 2)
Unio Mystica (Vol 1 & 2)
The Wisdom of the Sands (Vol 1 & 2)

TANTRA
Tantra: The Supreme Understanding

The Tantra Experience
The Royal Song of Saraha
(same as Tantra Vision, Vol 1)
The Tantric Transformation
The Royal Song of Saraha
(same as Tantra Vision, Vol 2)

TAO
The Empty Boat
The Secret of Secrets
Tao: The Golden Gate
Tao: The Pathless Path
Tao: The Three Treasures
When the Shoe Fits

THE UPANISHADS
Heartbeat of the Absolute
Ishavasya Upanishad
I Am That *Isa Upanishad*
Philosophia Ultima
Mandukya Upanishad
The Supreme Doctrine
Kenopanishad
Finger Pointing to the Moon
Adhyatma Upanishad
That Art Thou *Sarvasar Upanishad, Kaivalya Upanishad, Adhyatma Upanishad*
The Ultimate Alchemy *Atma Pooja Upanishad* (Vol 1 & 2)
Vedanta: Seven Steps to Samadhi
Akshaya Upanishad

WESTERN MYSTICS
Guida Spirituale
On the Desiderata
The Hidden Harmony
The Fragments of Heraclitus
The Messiah (Vol 1 & 2)
Commentaries on Kahlil Gibran's The Prophet
The New Alchemy: To Turn You On *Commentaries on Mabel Collins' Light on the Path*
Philosphia Perennis (Vol 1 & 2)
The Golden Verses of Pythagoras
Zarathustra:
A God That Can Dance
Zarathustra:
The Laughing Prophet
Commentaries on Nietzsche's Thus Spake Zarathustra

YOGA
Yoga: The Alpha and the Omega (Vol 1-10)
Yoga: The Science of the Soul (Vol 1-3) (same as Yoga: The Alpha and the Omega Vol 1-3)

ZEN AND ZEN MASTERS
Ah, This!
Ancient Music in the Pines
And the Flowers Showered
A Bird on the Wing
(same as Roots and Wings)
Bodhidharma: The Greatest Zen Master
Communism and Zen Fire, Zen Wind
Dang Dang Doko Dang
The First Principle
God is Dead: Now Zen is the Only Living Truth
The Grass Grows By Itself
The Great Zen Master Ta Hui
Hsin Hsin Ming: The Book of Nothing *Discourses on the Faith-Mind of Sosan*
1 Celebrate Myself: God is No Where, Life is Now Here
Kyozan: A True Man of Zen
Nirvana: The Last Nightmare
No Mind: The Flowers of Eternity
No Water, No Moon

One Seed Makes the Whole Earth Green
Returning to the Source
The Search: Talks on the 10 Bulls of Zen
A Sudden Clash of Thunder
The Sun Rises in the Evening
Take it Easy (Vol 1)
Poems of Ikkyu
Take it Easy (Vol 2)
Poems of Ikkyu
This Very Body the Buddha
Hakuin's Song of Meditation
Walking in Zen, Sitting in Zen
The White Lotus
Yakusan: Straight to the Point of Enlightenment
Zen Manifesto: Freedom From Oneself
Zen: The Mystery and the Poetry of the Beyond
Zen: The Path of Paradox (Vol 1, 2 & 3)
Zen: The Special Transmission

ZEN BOXED SETS

The World of Zen (5 volumes)
Live Zen
This. This. A Thousand Times This
Zen: The Diamond Thunderbolt
Zen: The Quantum Leap from Mind to No-Mind
Zen: The Solitary Bird, Cuckoo of the Forest

Zen: All The Colors Of The Rainbow (5 vols.)
The Buddha: The Emptiness of the Heart
The Language of Existence
The Miracle
The Original Man
Turning In

Osho: On the Ancient Masters of Zen (7 vols.)
Dogen: The Zen Master
Hyakujo: The Everest of Zen – With Basho's haikus
Isan: No Footprints in the Blue Sky
Joshu: The Lion's Roar
Ma Tzu: The Empty Mirror
Nansen: The Point Of Departure
Rinzai: Master of the Irrational
**Each volume is also available individually.*

RESPONSES TO QUESTIONS

Be Still and Know
Come, Come, Yet Again Come
The Goose is Out
The Great Pilgrimage: From Here to Here
The Invitation
My Way: The Way of the White Clouds
Nowhere to Go But In
The Razor's Edge
Walk Without Feet, Fly Without Wings and Think Without Mind
The Wild Geese and the Water
Zen: Zest, Zip, Zap and Zing

TALKS IN AMERICA

From Bondage To Freedom
From Darkness To Light
From Death To Deathlessness
From the False To the Truth
From Unconsciousness To Consciousness
The Rajneesh Bible (Vol 2-4)
The Rajneesh Upanishad

THE WORLD TOUR

Beyond Enlightenment
Talks in Bombay
Beyond Psychology
Talks in Uruguay
Light on the Path
Talks in the Himalayas
The Path of the Mystic
Talks in Uruguay
Sermons in Stones
Talks in Bombay
Socrates Poisoned Again After 25 Centuries
Talks in Greece
The Sword and the Lotus
Talks in the Himalayas
The Transmission of the Lamp
Talks in Uruguay

OSHO'S VISION FOR THE WORLD

The Golden Future
The Hidden Splendor
The New Dawn
The Rebel
The Rebellious Spirit

THE MANTRA SERIES

Hari Om Tat Sat
Om Mani Padme Hum
Om Shantih Shantih Shantih
Sat-Chit-Anand
Satyam-Shivam-Sundram

PERSONAL GLIMPSES

Books I Have Loved
Glimpses of a Golden Childhood
Notes of a Madman

INTERVIEWS WITH THE WORLD PRESS

The Last Testament (Vol 1)

INTIMATE TALKS BETWEEN MASTER AND DISCIPLE – DARSHAN DIARIES

A Rose is a Rose is a Rose
Be Realistic: Plan for a Miracle
Believing the Impossible Before Breakfast
Beloved of My Heart
Blessed are the Ignorant
Dance Your Way to God
Don't Just Do Something, Sit There
Far Beyond the Stars
For Madmen Only
The Further Shore
Get Out of Your Own Way
God's Got A Thing about You
God is Not for Sale
The Great Nothing
Hallelujah!
Let Go!
The 99 Names of Nothingness
No Book, No Buddha, No Teaching, No Disciple
Nothing to Lose but Your Head
Only Losers Can Win in This Game
Open Door
Open Secret
The Shadow of the Whip
The Sound of One Hand Clapping
The Sun Behind the Sun Behind the Sun
The Tongue-Tip Taste of Tao
This Is It
Turn On, Tune In and Drop the Lot
What Is, Is, What Ain't, Ain't
Won't You Join The Dance

COMPILATIONS

Bhagwan Shree Rajneesh: On Basic Human Rights

Jesus Crucified Again, This Time in Ronald Reagan's America

Priests and Politicians: The Mafia of the Soul

GIFT BOOKS OF OSHO QUOTATIONS

A Must for Contemplation Before Sleep

A Must for Morning Contemplation

Gold Nuggets

More Gold Nuggets

Words From a Man of No Words

At the Feet of the Master

PHOTOBOOKS

Shree Rajneesh: A Man of Many Climates, Seasons and Rainbows *through the eye of the camera*

Impressions... *Osho Commune International Photobook*

BOOKS ABOUT OSHO

Bhagwan: The Buddha for the Future *by Juliet Forman, S.R.N., S.C.M., R.M.N.*

Bhagwan Shree Rajneesh: The Most Dangerous Man Since Jesus Christ *by Sue Appleton, L.L.B. M.A.B.A.*

Bhagwan: The Most Godless Yet the Most Godly Man *by Dr. George Meredith, M.D. M.B.B.S. M.R.C.P.*

Bhagwan: One Man Against the Whole Ugly Past of Humanity *by Juliet Forman, S.R.N., S.C.M., R.M.N.*

Bhagwan: Twelve Days That Shook the World *by Juliet Forman, S.R.N. S.C.M., R.M.N.*

Was Bhagwan Shree Rajneesh Poisoned by Ronald Reagan's America? *by Sue Appleton, L.L.B. M.A.B.A.*

Diamond Days With Osho *by Ma Prem Shunyo*

GIFTS

Zorba the Buddha Cookbook

THE VISION FOR A NEW MAN

Notes